John Henry

Teri L. Tilwick

Boston, Massachusetts
Chandler, Arizona
Glenview, Illinois
Upper Saddle River, New Jersey

Illustrations
3, 4, 5, 6, 7, 8, 9, 10, 11, 13 Joanne Friar.

Photographs
Every effort has been made to secure permission and provide appropriate credit for photographic material.
The publisher deeply regrets any omission and pledges to correct errors called to its attention in subsequent editions.

Unless otherwise acknowledged, all photographs are the property of Pearson Education, Inc.

Photo locators denoted as follows: Top (T), Center (C), Bottom (B), Left (L), Right (R), Background (Bkgd)

Opener: Library of Congress; 1 Library of Congress; 2 Thinkstock; 12 Adeline Knapp, Overland Monthly, VOL xxxv, No 205, January 1900; 14 Library of Congress; 15 Library of Congress.

Copyright © 2013 by Pearson Education, Inc., or its affiliates. All rights reserved. Printed in the United States of America. This publication is protected by copyright, and permission should be obtained from the publisher prior to any prohibited reproduction, storage in a retrieval system, or transmission in any form by any means, electronic, mechanical, photocopying, recording, or likewise. For information regarding permissions, write to Pearson Curriculum Rights & Permissions, One Lake Street, Upper Saddle River, New Jersey 07458.

Pearson® is a trademark, in the U.S. and/or in other countries, of Pearson Inc. or its affiliates.

ISBN-13: 978-0-328-67587-6
ISBN-10: 0-328-67587-3

11 12 13 14 V0SI 18 17 16 15

Have you visited a **national** park?
Thank John Muir.
He helped start the national parks.

Muir was born in Scotland long ago.
He loved to be outdoors.

Muir's family sailed to America.
He and his brother were very happy.

Muir moved to a farm in Wisconsin.
He had a pony named Jack.

Muir was an **inventor**.
He invented clever machines.

Muir showed his machines.
Many people came to see them.

Muir went to college.
He learned about nature.

Muir invented a useful desk.
It helped him to study.

Muir left college and got a job.
He hurt his eye and had to quit.

Then Muir took a nature walk.
He **hiked** a thousand miles.

Muir then went to California.
He lived in Yosemite Valley.

He wanted people to see nature.
He began a club to protect nature.

President Theodore Roosevelt visited.
He and Muir hiked together.

Roosevelt helped start national parks.
Muir helped make it happen.

Glossary

hiked walked through nature

inventor someone who makes something new

national belonging to everyone in the country